EXCAVATIONS

Excavations

NEAL MASON

PETERLOO POETS

First published in 1991
by Peterloo Poets
2 Kelly Gardens, Calstock, Cornwall PL18 9SA, U.K.

British Library Cataloguing in Publication Data
Mason, Neal
  Excavations.
  I. Title
  823.914

  ISBN 1-871471-17-6

Printed in Great Britain by
Latimer Trend & Company Ltd, Plymouth

ACKNOWLEDGEMENTS are due to the editors of the following journals and anthologies: *Poetry Review, Encounter, Keltica (U.S.A.), Newbury Competition Anthology, Spectrum, Envoi, Poetry Wales, Frames, University College of Wales Competition Anthologies, The Anglo-Welsh Review, Planet, Lines Review, 2 Plus 2, Window on Wales, Scottish National Competition Anthology, Ambit.*

Eight of the poems in this volume were represented in *Peterloo Preview 2* (1990).

Published with the support of the Welsh Arts Council.

Supported by

Cornwall
County Council

WITH THE ASSISTANCE OF

SOUTH WEST ARTS

Recipient of an Arts Council Incentive Funding Award

To R.H.

Contents

Roman Sandal

When your midnight came
you left
no fancy slipper to fashion
comfortable tales; only this
buckled leather
scuffed and kicked off
last thing at night.

I stop
as though tripped,
straggling thongs
arranged in ornamental sand,
two thousand years
between one step
and the next.

The indentation
of a toe. Silly
to be alarmed
by scraps of mouldy leather,
wrinkled and worn,
about size nine, yet
how perfectly it fits.

Mirrored in the case
like a buyer in a shoe shop
I read of workers
brushing carefully at your heels,
my track shoes faster
by an inch or two
when unearthed in the dig.

Arms Museum

A montage of styles, Tudor to present,
its appearance alarms, so I reconnoitre
the outside first. A model of a soldier, gestalt
harlequin of opaque diamonds, stands guard
behind leaded glass, a challenging proto-cubist.
The Georgian window detaches him, rational
as building blocks, dimple for a heart,
while the sash window, First War, quarters
the man, a pane distorting his face. But,
at the modern wing, a sheet of armoured plate
glass, I abruptly realise he's too figurative,
not a model at all, and reflect
that, this glass broken, the complete image
will be lost.

Terracotta Mouse c. 2,000 B.C.

I don't think my cat
would give you a second glance.
Calling in while Christmas shopping
I thought I heard tiny claws
scratching on glass. Survivor
from a Bronze Age childhood
I can't quite recall, you toy
with curiosity, your tail-less
comfortable lump cruelly trapped
in a display case. You appear lost,
crouch timidly as though puzzled
by where they've all gone,
those tiny hands that rounded
sharp ears, look at me
reprovingly, as if I'd abandoned you
ages ago, never again to be hidden
among cheeses, or in a parent's bed.
But now I must go
and buy plastic toys, probably broken
by Easter, for children who'll leave me
in a place too orderly for mice,
or my cat, and occasionally call in
while shopping, to see me
gazing from a window, trapped by glass.

Cartology

Bleached and torn folds of the map,
dandelion seeds slipping through summer
to take root between place-names,
obscure. designated footpaths
and overgrow a pencil-lined route.

Interrogated the map
while leaves rattled on the grid
sieving debris for the next series,
the dry russet shapes' emaciation
not depicted in the symbols.

Rain spattered the colours
from clouds above the contours,
droplets dissolving valleys, trickles
coursing down plotted rivers
whose banks didn't burst to scale.

Opened the sheet on the ground,
smoothing out creases, peaks
and hills just before snowflakes
levelled and blotted features, drifting highest
where the legend showed arid desert.

Cigarette burns in the sea,
torn mountains, cup-rings through towns,
no words on the landscape
to explain, the map dumped in a bin
where insects traverse it with ease.

Bronze Age Board Game
Bi-facial, c.2,500 B.C.

I play a game, a guessing game,
your faceless forehead creased
confronting me across the board.
I seek you out, your hidden moves
a ploy for time that merely adds
four thousand, five hundred years
to five minutes.

Rich enough for leisure, you can afford
to gamble clues. Artefacts all around,
statically displayed, you move in shadows
cast by an ancient hearth. I see children
concealing yawns to push bedtime back
a space and, most games for pairs, a wife
puzzling you from my position now.
Perhaps I cheat. This brooch, dull gold
hoarding firelight, might as well be hers,
each a prize won on a bigger board.
Animal skins—one of them, alive,
gnaws complacently at a bone, teeth-marks
still visible—lie scattered like bodies
on the floor, more than darkness perhaps
closing in outside. Consider your position.
En prise you sip from a goblet,
not yet dented, take fruit from vases,
prospective shards filled to overflowing
by a proud, subjected race; slaves
you move like pieces.

Suddenly—a surprise attack—
time sweeps the board, angry at intrusion.
A fluorescent light flickers
cold fire, the only movement to escape
from ranks of cabinets. I move
sadly away, my loss too great
even to guess at.

Rubbish Tip Sunset

Colours littered
under an orange-peel sky.
A few minutes recycle rubbish
into silhouette, intriguing shapes
like a cross on a mound
caught in dying light. The body
of a doll, flung limbs embracing
dirt, rests its head on stones, withered
peelings a travesty of flowers.
A towel, incongruously folded, drapes
a mud-filled washing machine, dabs up
glimmers from briefly re-illumined
light bulbs. Wine bottles pour out a puddle,
a chalice sipped by rodents, walked on
by water boatmen as an over-ripe sun
sinks in the miasma. Claws scratch
the dusk for alms of mildewed bread,
leaf through paper, the word
redundant as early stars sprinkle
evening like salt over pottage.

First Flowers

Last April's aroma of blossom
transported me nowhere
near as much as this stone bouquet,
its one hundred and thirty-six
million year old petals colourless,
scentless, but more heady
than first-flowering spring.

Still fresh, a fossilized recollection
tugs, as though I'd been there, at unpicked
stalks and buds waiting to be pressed,
a postponed wonder which blooms
now, as it did in a grey-green world,
flora itself young, a surprise of petals
pre-empting every poet, every lover.

I offer you these, heavy and slate-grey,
years too late, as a spray
of yellows, reds and blues, a token to all
that might have grown,
seeded in early sunshine, nurtured
by imagination and ever-fertile hope.

Rite

A collection at the door; inside
a mystery of music and lights,
the celebrants in leather vestments
gyrate in coloured smoke, intone
between exhalations, mingling
with their own shadows.

Then the sacrificial virgin.

More disturbing than physical desire,
strange arms reach out for her,
true intentions disguised. Beginning
her dance, she whirls excitedly
through incense, her movements free,
unformulated till, having spilled
the libation, the selected one
stands before her.

The pace slows, grows deliberate
and entangled in arms, ritual phrases
exchanged while she counters the groping,
the proper interval being observed.

Outside, the night is cold,
encourages them closer. She seems happy,
almost careless, her dancing-shoes
dangerous on the ice, a procession
of two initiates, parallel tracks
leading from Saturday night
to Saturday morning, new mysteries,
irresistible and fresh, despite the familiar
march and worn stone aisle.

Easter Island

Easter Island, trinity
of extinct volcanoes, barren
rock from whose altars
the suspicion of slaughter drips
like rain off a leaf, trickles
through history's canopy
as a stream might thread hills.

But there are no streams, no rivers,
no canopies of leaves.
Trees that might have shaded
the statues, their stone trunks
prolific in an arid landscape,
fed a conflagration long ago,
the flames casting myriad
fighting shadows whose charred bones
choke a mass grave at Poike Ditch.

Each silent statue
faces inwards, contemplates this island
called the Navel of the World, peers
through gaps in missing branches
at missing people
whose stone picks, dropped suddenly
as though red hot, still await
their owners, the last and greatest statue
unfinished, still fixed to its rock,
a Promethean figure perhaps.

No longer venerated, except
by archaeologists who, faces impervious
as rock, can measure extinction precisely,
the great stone ghosts, figureheads
on an island Marie Celeste, watch
tourists drift in from the volcanic
island of the world, their backs turned
on the threatening, endless ocean.

Final Comic Strip

FRAME 1
Funny
how you cavort, inflate your ideas,
profoundest thoughts, into simple
two-dimensional bubbles, shiny
yet reflective, ephemeral
parodies that mock
the hand that creates you.

FRAME 2
What scrape
will you romp through this week,
amusement your chief concern? You pose,
ridiculous attitudes, hilarious
as one thing after another, irresponsible
pranks safely framed from
surrounding world news.

FRAME 3
Your logic
diverting, you get it all wrong, leap
from frame to frame, full colour
disasters obligatory as narrative,
so very amusing; how we laugh
to see you mangled,
blown up, incinerated.

FRAME 4
Torn
but still grinning, late
edition long out of date, you amuse
empty pavements, unswept gutters,
frolic in a windblown puddle, nearby
billboard an epitaph, caption
no-one will read.

$E = MC^2$

In the particle accelerator of the mind
thought circles endlessly, ever faster
as concentration is applied, until
the point is reached when more effort
merely increases the mass of the thought.

Strained beyond the everyday, logic
appears to bend, buckles as it supports
contradictory philosophies, proves time
subject to gravity, destroys itself like sound
turning into heat, or matter becoming energy.

Yet, each morning, the eight-ten arrives and
we work our slow way to inevitability,
enervating as we go, equating hope
with reason, until the final destination
rushes into sight at frightening speed.

Oddly comforting to know even Einstein
couldn't make his marriage work, that love
is a quantum leap, the mundane unfathomable
as the cosmic. And, as the rational becomes fantastic,
even belief might prove reasonable.

Spinster

I can afford to be swindled
in the village shop; a bargain
that buys silence. I cycle
at quiet times, but you're always there
smirking, reducing me as I purchase
whatever's twopence off, to a bag
of nerves loading panniers,
trying to retain some balance.

My awkwardness affronting
something deep within you, I speak
only when spoken to, discount
half you say—thus adding
to my crimes—and your children's
hurled insults rattling in spokes,
my face red with exertion, perhaps,
as I ride my broom (will you never tire
of that joke?) to a home I hope's moved
out of town. Terrified of sentiment,
you censured my cat, black, still
cowering in ditches, its careful affection
some comfort against insinuations,
lonely, sexual, painful as parody
or the sharp elbow of derision.

But sometimes, when you sleep
or make love, I escape to the past
and haunt, witch-like, a corner
you turned long ago. Always
punctual, unlike him, I conjure up
long lost laughter, lumpy hopes
back thirty years and slim, an entranced
callow girl scorning rumours
she was mere currency. I gave
everything for a spellbinding future,

its promise secure as a loan
to a valued friend, and heard
the chink of wedding bells
growing ever louder; heard them still
when the embryo was spent
in the clinic where my illness was born.

Like his wife and valued friends, I thought
I could afford to be flattered, but you
were my convalescence, draining
all my reserves. You joke
about witches' sabbaths, unaware
the sky's too black, too heavy
for flight, though clouds race, deft
as yesterday, across a spendthrift moon,
bright and round as a coin.
My wheels hiss home, pass your dark
houses, locked and mercifully quiet, pass
your cars and village shop
glowing with welcome and family bargains
I'll never be able to afford.

To R

Your absence
Echoes in my letterbox,
The many things we should have said
Scan only in my imagination,
The perfect postman.

Every morning is without you;
I clamber down daybreak to the door
And feel emptiness,
Already penning the day's letter
As though replying to yours.

So I re-read the days we had,
The distance between us increasing
Beyond the reach of any stamp;
I address you
Knowing only where you used to be.

Sunset, the Ruins of Bradenstoke Abbey, Wiltshire, April 1982

If I had words
I'd call out to you.

In this long, lonely silence
Only the breeze is eloquent.
The horizon for a fulcrum
The setting sun prizes evening
Off the ruins.
Those who sense a presence here
Are seeking footprints on stony ground;
My footprints are everywhere.

Listen
And I'll call to you.

Key-stones, columns, foundations;
A scattered jig-saw puzzle
In whose picture I featured too.
Alert only to danger
The rabbit and the vole play
In the footsteps of processions;
A congregation of birds sings here now
To a future that keeps returning.

And why are you here—You
Whose company doubles isolation?

You covet more than this abbey's sunset.
Fallen stones lie pillowed on grass
But you do not rest.
Hidden from the sun
Shadows pivot on columns and walls
Without ever seeing what manipulates them.
Absent-mindedly you kick the stones
As though trying to recall.

Just out of hearing
I call to you.

No longer does stained glass
Restrict the view;
Empty windows stare in disbelief
At vespers in the countryside,
Where sacrifice was never outmoded
And experiment never crystalised
Into creed. These ruins
Were but a temporary home.

You can hear me now;
You have always heard me.

This new night seems darker
Than the last.
The abbey blocks out stars,
Arrogates the centre of attention to itself,
Just as it always did.
But I am crumbling the stones,
Dismantling the ghosts; soon
Few will be puzzled by ruins.

Trigonometry

You stood there, the sun
biting your shoulder, my sunglasses
reflecting in the lens. As though
holding a theodolite, you fixed
me in relation to you, your shadow
leaning on my arm. You paused.
We've been still ever since.

Finger on the button
we surveyed each other by turns,
the distance between us
a base, the leafy scenery dotted
with personal reference points.
But your shadow moved
away; the sun floated free.

These snaps—mere contour maps
of Arcady—are slightly blurred; perhaps,
one day, we'll speak them into focus,
those natural features
in our emotional geography.
Their surfaces reflect
drab light from my window.

At this moment maybe
you too are studying them. We look
two dimensional. Never mind.
Irrespective of distance,
frames, angles or limits, we'll
triangulate a meeting-point,
the vertex in the sky.

Vehicle Deck

Fixed on our grid
with nowhere to race to,
our vision limited
by a bulkhead horizon,
we bank and sway
in unison, lean
for the sea bends
as though vying for positions
we can't alter.

We speed ahead,
handbrakes fully applied,
steering-wheels obstinate
to commands, the grey-green
camouflaged armour
like sculpted sea water,
every dial at rest
waiting, impassive,
despite our strain.

Diesels rumble deep
below, the powers that propel us
as though individual effort
were a spurious thing. Suspension
grumbles to itself as if
a chained neighbour could collide
while, outside, the threat
of total shipwreck looms,
all-encompassing as the sea.

Never hurt scenery ...

Never hurt scenery
the way it hurts now,
dragged the beach
inland, broke waves,
carved our initials
on flawless summer skies;
yet how they glower today.

Waves, tetchy, fling
your absence shoreward,
winter glaring bare
contempt, our sun's
beachball falling
from the blue; sunshine
I should have caught.

New Departures

Archaeopteryx, before it could fly,
floundered in its useless feathers
like some Jurassic joke, a floozy,
provocative as it flounced for predators,
unlikely to outpace extinction.

Preening intelligence, we display
love of achievement but, in church,
can't believe in it. Clever enough to pollute
air missiles might fly through, we look up
and admire birds in the sky.

Like a child with too many toys
we'd be happier with less, but time
flies, Peter Pan unlikely
as a static kite; a new jet roars overhead
and a boy's model 'planes change shape.

But his dreams travel faster than light.
First it was Icarus, a mere boy
of an idea; then Leonardo's wings spanning
centuries, the concept light years ahead
of events. We must fly. We have somewhere to go.

The image of Man on Voyager
is no-one we know; a Platonic form's
faltering first steps in space, the flight
of painful consciousness the forerunner
to a new departure.

Ram on a Mountainside

At the foot of the escarpment
I nearly stumble over you,
a shaggy off-white wet patch
dead among the rocks.

I project the curve of your fall,
see you back up there chewing,
your wool angry at the wind
as rain buries into you; but your face,
now split open to the weather,
complacent.

Nearby a busy stream impels
itself between littered boulders,
loops evasively round you.

As always at these places
precipitate rubbish there before you,
unburied reminders an ever-present scar;
an old mattress, not sound enough
to land on, its springs a parody
of your skew horns, mocks
your sprawled sleep.

Gaping at your wasted head
I wonder which grey patch misjudged,
which part, eager for that extra mouthful,
pushed you one step too far, and
was convinced that this dead ram
could never be you.

Second Frost

Splintered by bare branches
an ice cold moon sheens
through the window, lays my
shadow in the empty cot
while I and the dimming fire
settle into ourselves, the ashen moonlight
still aglow near the grate.

Frozen ferns cobweb the bank,
clouds immobile in the stiff air,
the secret ministry of frost
crystallizing my abstraction
through whose chill silence I,
unlike Coleridge, hear no gentle breathing,
and silence too is an echo.

Thought warms to summer nights:
a bat, its signals always seeking
itself; two strangers recognising
each other's awe at the sunset,
finding personal cloud-pictures,
catching phrases from nature's eternal language
and rendering them their own way.

The malleable summer air
shrinks back into the grate; bars
of moonshadow stripe the cot;
an owlet's cry—and a second
in search of the first—skates
the silvered darkness that reflects faithful images,
permanent as frost.

Eskimo Child

Young, snow-blind
with inexperience, I wonder
about trees and the colour green
a trapper traded us for furs.
Father says I've seen them, held
twigs in my hand, but he's wary
of the trapper, the harpoon
that needs no throwing, ice
shivering at the noise. I wondered
whether he'd shot all the trees.

Fat with tales, he talked
far beyond snow, stories so colourful
they hurt my eyes. Even father
looked away, his lore of kayaks
and skin tents made mean by boats
big as icebergs, grey igloos
that never melt, boneless fish
trawled with baskets in super-fertile
markets; a wash of words, green
rare as chilled air.

I asked again, impatient
of garish myths, my horizon
bleached, except for specks of blood and fur
and the subtlety of what the sun does.
He sped on, losing me
in acres of leaves with fruit
like giant raindrops—surely a harvest
of fantasy—to camp-fire fables of concrete
snugger than fur, confined grass
and a people harder than ice.

Older now, wary
of encroaching sales talk, I wonder
about trees and the colour green
they traded for clouds of smoke.
My icy habitat shrinks, trapped
by mining companies who burn
the future as soon as the past,
my incredulous son wondering
about the colour blue
and the soot that falls like snow.

ECT

Electrodes like Walkman earphones,
shoes off, feet up, the silence
on tiptoes, wary.

Even music
had become a noise, a slow wading
through indifference thick as treacle,
meaningless conversation
mouthed behind glass, so the pre-med

wasn't far to travel.
A captive audience of one,
months of neglected music
queuing up like old friends
come to view the body;
an injection to immobilise
limbs, as though hands
cared enough to clap.

A few electrifying seconds
curl toes rigid, the silent music
exhilarating, so good
every muscle wants to conduct it,
strains jerking tendons
on a wilful marionette.

Afterwards, sleep sings
a too soothing lullaby, distracts
from the whir of re-winding
spools, gives way to dance, inviting
from a swept and polished floor.

The shops look bright,
pedestrians with a spring in their step,
street-smiles with no sharp edges,
words without dissonance,
the whole grubby hubbub
in harmony, invisible earphones playing
even hurt at a jaunty pace.

But yesterday
wasn't like that. It's walked out
and taken the tapes with it.

Garreg-Lwyd

Here, dispersed in mist,
time treats the boulders gently,
scarcely acknowledging my presence.
Of what use is time up here?
As though I could tell it
by the movement of the rocks.
I wander the ages,
the particular left in the valley
where, like perfection, it seems unlikely.
But I recollect the Age of Gold
and watch for its return.

Robed in ancient vestments,
countryside shining in armour, I hid
from the Second Augustan Legion
as it hacked at our mythology, spears
glinting in my eyes while I
warded off history with a song.

The fresh wind is persistent;
unobstructed by bush or tree
it mines rock from quarries,
small clouds of sheep roaming
grass-top high, eating, excreting,
forever recycling the mountain.

Arthur, wish-fulfilment
or archetypal saviour, this time
from Saxons, might have ridden by
below, but gouged a legend so deep
the dust obscured him, speeches
chichés, enemies dragons,
and all the while Celtic saints
intimating eternity—different
from the Augustinian
the other side of Offa's Dyke. But I
knew better than to descend.

Fitzhamon won't foray today
chain-mailed against the weather.
He scans the scenery, his eyes
feet-thick loopholes, embrasures
in a desire to conquer. But up here
where creation almost forgot to come,
there's little care the weather doesn't bring.
I watch the castle at Carreg Cennen
grow stronger below, offering
protection, but I shelter among cairns,
prefer the safety of exposure
while Edward castellates the clouds,
makes battlements of skylines,
Glyndwr's roars of defiance
floating like a harmless mist
along the valley floor.

I heard singing
drift up from chapels, calling
me to join them, the air
wrung of other sounds, but then
a bird called
and Methodism just evaporated
like so much morning dew.

Even industry failed
to smoke me out. I watched
its slow retreat, grass
creeping after it, awkward angles
settling into something more comfortable,
the Beacons shifting
from purple to baked orange,
just as they always did
before there was history.

I wait for the new Era
of Gold, imagination
a colourful festival,
not a necessity, certain
the day will come when
I can return to the valley.

Für Alicia

I do not trust myself
with words, in case I damage
them by rough handling, offer you
these like fragile shells
to hold to your ear, knowing
silence would be worse.

The sea sings, drowns
each shallow syllable perhaps
better left unsaid, such safety
in silence, yet you drift so
lonely on an alien shore, waves
deafening as they crash.

Barefoot you pick your way
drowning in seagull screams,
the empty horizon hissing
like a huge shell, shingle
tingling in your ears,
tearing at your feet.

Far away I speak rain
and mouth in the wind which sucks
at sound, shout a dumb-show,
my expressions buffeted through air,
our turbulent sea-spray shapes
flung at each other's feet.

Where else to find you but close
to the edge?—wandering where ground slides
and silence crashes again and again
washing words away, tangled
as seaweed before torn apart
by an uncaring, impersonal tide.

Cetacea

From the end of the ocean
a cry
shrill and plaintive,
a sonic search in the world of water,
a green sound growing
with its echo, pulsing through seaweed
and silver shoals.

And on to acres
of lazy liquid blue
lacerated on coral, treacling upwards
towards an amoeboid sun.

The call
cutting through sharp water, cold
and brittle in blue and white,
striking sparks off ice in crystal chasms,
seeking expression
of absolute clarity.

Down
and compressed to depths,
a world with no weather
but slow-motion breezes, to wrecks
oceans old and silted, voice pipes
to dark compartments waiting
in awed silence for orders
that will never come.

The cry
not stifled by effluent or rubbery bubbles,
seeking the pipes and looking in,
bumping lethargic lumps of wood
dipping irritably
as in sleep.

The sound slipping
with the sands of every shore,
curling with breakers,
wading up beaches
and foaming as it speaks, salty
in the mouths of bathers,
each drop a paraphrase,

an urgent plea
from unnumbered noises of the seas
to the deaf on land.

Skipping down . . .

Skipping down youthful hillsides
like a flock of woolly-brained lambs
we frisked and played, revelled
in unexplored country, fresh views still
not eroded by outlook when,
suddenly and linked to no fence,
the gate.

Solitary in acres of purple-green
it commanded attention like a monolith
or totem, gave our games focus
other than pleasure, yet seemed
to restrict the view; it stood
at a confluence of well-worn tracks,
trampled grass fanned out—a magnetic
field—by droves of plodding feet
funnelled from nowhere to nowhere
circuitously.

Drawn towards it
as though it barred our progress
we stared at the prospect beyond,
its formal layout, constrained paths,
grey slopes.

Some of us turned away, content
to lollop in the marsh, climbed
natural outcrops of rock, the sunshine
our playmate, no threat
on the horizon to overshadow us.

But when, later, stung by rain
from tongues of disapproving cloud
and harassed by snarling storms
we raced homeward via the gate

we found it locked.

The Ring

The storm breaks. Spears of wet light
glance off tarmac, penetrate ranks
of children, their shrieks drowned
by advancing waves of thunder, a hail
of cold missiles slapping each hand.

Her sign instructing weather,
the Lollipop Lady guides them, a Valkyrie
in white plastic armour, hair streaming
in wind as puddles sprawl at her feet,
the zebra-crossing for a rainbow bridge.

Assembly takes place in a great hall
obviously built by giants. They sing
hymns conducted by demi-gods, gold
trophies glittering like tomorrow, a prize
to be won. Lightning fires its warning.

The children wonder why gods
have such a need to pray, but playtime
soon comes, and goes, the call to lie
down dead a persistent motif, copies
from the real world of immortal masters.

Laughing at the future, the Norns' rope
a toy to skip with to fire drill,
they line up, twilit, knowing their inheritance
can't really burn, distant thunder
circling like a foe. The storm breaks.

The danger ...

The danger of another dawn threatens.
Red morning
Glints on bedroom windows,
Picks its targets
As though through infra-red sights.
Well trained, man moves quickly;
Armed with a newspaper he runs
From breakfast to bus-shelter,
Boards, fights off the unacceptable;
Hands wave aside
All but the manual labour of living.
Gaining the objective
He makes for his office,
Parries 'Good mornings' with his own,
Drinks coffee in the respite.
After lunch
The attrition of the afternoon;
Repetition wards off thought
Except in those sudden, silent moments
when the mind seems undefended.
Eyes glaze
While inner ears prick up,
Nerves tauten
At a vague fear stalking unseen,
Until office exigencies prevail again.
Homecoming
Draws the thread back across the frame
Weaving, not protection,
But greater vulnerability,
The colours of approaching dusk
Unable to camouflage the human shape.
Meanwhile
Heaven's eye perfects its aim.

Strange Exile

She hasn't travelled
Where her thoughts have been,
Nor run her fingers over far off lands,
But the place she lives in few have seen
For few seek society
In desert sands.
Strange city
Built inside her head,
Strange state
Whose subject she's become;
What pointless compass led her there
Beyond the bounds of everyone?
Disused tracks lead away from the city
To ghost-towns she used to call home;
Their urbanity was comfortable enough,
But all roads led to Rome.
The streets are laid down in circles
And not one building proclaims its name,
For the church and the library, the museum and the home
Have the same facade of the same grey stone.
The windows are sham—they're all mirrors;
She gazes out upon her cerebral scene
Watching life that's already passed by,
Seeing, not where it's leading,
But where it's been.
At night she plays music which echoes round
The empty streets;
Her laughter fills the air
For, though one is missed, she fêtes
The thousands who aren't there.
But autonomy, ambassador of war,
Offends the empire whose subjects acclaim
The sovereignty of convention;
She knows she must arm,
She knows she must fight;
The outcast must cast the invader out
Once again.

On Icknield Way

I crawl from the earth's womb,
a Neolithic birth climbing
out of Grime's Graves, chalk dust written
on my skin like messages, directions
I'm compelled to follow. I knap
flints into weapons against
the coming years, sharp axes
to knock history into shape, and head
for the Icknield Way, trade route for bartering
lives, wring the best rate
from whatever I must buy with
my time.

By Thetford I was dead.
Wolves, disease, robbers; no record
to tell; as a nation, already
a failure. I must still be there
somewhere, vague particles
written on the chalk, an embryonic
need caught mid-stride on its way
out of Breckland. I needn't have lived
this time.

It was I who buried
the Mildenhall Treasure, a fourth century
panic preserved in silver, eyes shining
with greed, when light glinted
on other metal, swords that drove me
past tumuli, already old, like
bruises on a battered landscape, the burden
of missing silver weighing heavily
on my mind. At least
my passing left some record,
in time.

I arrived on Telegraph Hill,
reached Christianity, the views
expansive as we Saxons built
an abbey to murdered Alban, looked
back like awed spectators
in the theatre where Rome
defeated itself long ago.
But we built without stone,
our wooden faith fired
by our own internecine wars,
golden hair in flames, and Wessex,
a future destination, ran me through
in a skirmish, my last words curses
spilt on the cross of Icknield Way
and Watling Street, extant intersections
of time.

After the Conquest I was so poor
I ate salmon every day
filched from the Thames near Wallingford,
resented Benedictine monks grown fat
on self-denial; and I was hungry
to find a mate, attracted to
the west, yet failed once more, seemed
destined to starve, fight or fall
every time.

I left the track
in the fifteenth century, rode the White Horse
Hills, distant Stonehenge jolting
some prehistoric memory
I couldn't quite recall, then glimpsed
my first sight of her, hills rounded
as breasts, killed one of her ancestors
and watched Glendower stagger
bleeding into history, took her
by rape, and used her more than
one time.

She was beautiful, if wild, the womb
to return to, so I forced a marriage
in 1536, our union stormy
as Welsh weather. We retained
our own names and customs, and middle age
was the loneliest death of all, she
lost in her solitary nature,
accusing me of cruelty and neglect, turned
to Methodism, while I succumbed
to Puritanism after
a time.

A correct Victorian,
I arrived by rail, metal road
to ever-expanding empire, my
wooing more industrious,
each penetration of her collied womb
subjecting her, exhausting her,
parts all mine, the rest proud
as mountains and as distant,
though she satisfied a need at
the time.

Now I drive up the M4,
court you with new technology, fumble
with your words. We contend
with the problems of our age, yet still fight
old battles, not forgiving
the mistakes of youth, you nursing
your hurt, our only child, whose path
may follow a trampled route. Maybe
it's not too late to get on
the right track, talk about reconciliation,
about new directions and
about time.

Album

We viewed him each holiday
like time-lapse photography,
watched his portrait fill out
while we, shrinking slowly,
altered positions in chairs.

This one's out of focus,
except for his eyes, frozen
like a still life, but he seemed O.K.,
the master's favourite, so I don't know
why he was serious, distant.

He sent these of girlfriends—we
forget their names—at training college;
they passed quickly in and out
of frames, so we filed them in
the album we keep by the video.

These blank pages are because
he travelled, he said, lost
his camera so sent postcards,
the landscapes desolate, his writing
shaky due to illness or something.

Here he is at his first job—our last
snapshot before the tragedy—but
smiling for once, the boy with him
his favourite pupil who looks
terribly serious, distant.

The holiday brochure . . .

The holiday brochure shines
its sixty watt reflection on his skin,
dank suburbs forgotten as he basks
by a glossy blue sea, pours a glass
of pure spring water from a bottle,
twopence off at Sainsbury's, lays himself down
like a bath-towel on a beach.

The mountains stretch away
far beyond the battered chair, the grey
smoke-filled room cloudless
as distant eagles whirl
slowly round the lampshade;
when he wants an olive, he need only
reach out and pick one.

Too hot with both bars on
he leans to switch one off, feels the heat
beating his face while, down in the street,
a mule train plods past, hot sand
simmering the sound, golden granules
soft to his touch as liquid sunlight
or a shag-pile rug.

Curled against the cold his threadbare cat
sleeps on unaware of wolves baying
from beyond the divan, the snow-capped
mantelpiece echoing their calls as the sun
sinks back into its brochure;
outside a cold clatter of milk bottles
rattling on the doorstep of night.

Transport Café

At about latitude fifty-three
she sizzles fry-ups, chill morning rain
spattering the car park like fat
in a frying-pan. Eyes tired, her greasy gaze
slides down postcard-covered walls, pauses
at a saucy one from Brighton, a cloudless
view of Dieppe, curled edges of the Hook
browning in steam. By latitude forty-five
the bacon needs turning.
A reversing artic' elbows fog, parks
its reflection in a puddle. Droplets
of fat drip off Corfu onto the Algäuer Alps,
tarnished snow perspiring, condensation
thawing, the rivulets trickling across
a blistering Algerian sunset
and collecting on cans of Coke.
Rows of tanned weeks, none of them hers,
dazzle like a Mediterranean sun, carefree
colours spread out to bathe, date stamps
collecting an ever-deepening patina. She cooks
eggs, sunny side up, butters toast
in the shade of the Parthenon, pinned askew,
tilting dangerously towards the rolls.
Passing drivers dash off greetings, words
cursory as cards, breath scrawled on the cold
morning like spray from Atlantic rollers,
sandstorms in Morocco, salt
sprinkled over chips. The Adriatic boils
as she fills a teapot, the urn emitting
a raincloud to engulf most of Europe.
At lunchtime she sips muddy coffee, pretends
it's wine, relaxes at a pavement café
somewhere in the Auvergne, the afternoon
delivering more drivers, sunshine
easing through the clouds, a pale copy
of its continental self.

An aerial view of Venice sinks
behind the orangeade, low gears shaking
St. Marks down to latitude forty. More
beans and chips. More mugs of grey tea.
Walled in by vistas, she longs for summer,
looks forward to the guest-house
in Morecambe which beckons
like the promise of a distant land.

Atmospherics

Two thousand feet up
on the Beacons, head in the clouds, I
place my transistor on a rock.
Full volume it hurls messages
into the valley, acoustic torrents
welling from a two inch speaker,
the soft babble of a nearby stream
drowning it. Tiny waves of sound
batter limestone, world news squeaking
at endless hushing grass, a cool breeze
taking the announcer's breath away.
At three paces I can't hear
gunfire or cries for help,
gossip or adverts, the cadence
of the F.T. Index, nor what strength
on the Beaufort Scale this breeze
should measure; the sun shines
unforecast, ignores
the metallic incantation while
sheep chuckle at the Pastoral humming
to itself, or Götterdämmerung thundering
at its few inches of lichen, until
batteries droop, Dali-like, over
impervious rock, or a shower dissolves
the Water Music, the box mute
as surrounding scree. I turn,
stare down through mist at toy cars,
picture-book villages and silent
pedestrians, retrace my steps
and clutch the radio to me. There was
a time when I'd have left it.